I'm Bleeding!
School Health Humor
by
J.M. Handlos

Illustrated by
Brinley and Julie Conn

Confidentiality is always of upmost importance.
The names in the vignettes have been changed.

****

For school nurses and the students

in their care.

ACKNOWLEDGEMENTS

A special thanks to two of my granddaughters,
Brinley and Julie,
who illustrated this book
and
to other family members for
their assistance.

Prologue

Anyone who has ever worked with children can tell you that they often say exactly what is on their minds and, as we often mention in schools, repeat what they hear. This can be awkward for parents and can be equally difficult for school staff. This is especially true because, in some instances, it is not uncommon for children to misinterpret what they hear. It also has the potential to lead to some comical exchanges. In my case, comical exchanges in a school health room.

I worked as a school nurse for twenty-five years. The majority of my time in schools was spent working in elementary schools and preschools. I would often share my funny encounters with students with some of the office staff. After about ten to fifteen years I thought I should really start to write down some of the student comments in order to look back at some point in time for a good laugh.

I recently retired and decided to sit down and share some school health humor. Welcome to a little piece of school nursing!

I'm Bleeding!

A third grader walked into the health room holding up her hand with only her middle finger extended. I might have been the only person in the school who would not be offended by this action. I knew it meant that she had a cut on her finger, and indeed she had. She immediately told me, "I'm bleeding!"

Saving face

One of the more physically mature fifth grade boys came to the health room after lunch complaining that his jaw hurt.

Student: "It hurts so bad that I can't even eat."

Me: "Did you eat lunch?"

Student hesitates and responds: "Yes." He quickly adds, "I was kicked by my sister."

I started to wonder if this was a case where children were not supervised at home and perhaps I needed to see if an older sibling was involved.

Me: "How old is your sister?"

Student: "Three." He sheepishly continues, "But she is really strong."

Trying to find parents

I worked in a community near a military installation, and it was important to try to determine where a parent might work before trying to contact them. A number of parents were deployed overseas and there were also some local companies who were not fond of having employees pulled off an assembly line to take a phone call. I generally asked the children which parent they thought I should call and where the parent worked. In one case the exchange went like this:

Child: "You should call my dad."

Me: "Where does your dad work?"

The child proceeded to walk around the health room for about five minutes describing turns to make and buildings and fences you go past to get to the place of work. All the while I was waiting to try to determine if this was someone I should try to contact, and if I would eventually find out where the dad worked. The child suddenly stopped, and I thought I was finally going to get the answer to my question.

Child: "Oh wait, maybe he changed jobs."

It's just mom

Another strategy I would use to ensure that I was contacting the correct parent was to ask students what their parent's name was. I asked a kindergarten student what his mom's name was. He immediately informed me, "I don't think she has a real name, just mom."

On another occasion when verifying a kindergartner's mom's name, I asked the student, "How do you say your mom's name?" She said, "Actually, I just spell it M-O-M."

Identity crisis

Frequently there were students with the same first name in a classroom. Teachers would often have the students' names on their desks to identify their desk and help them learn the spelling of their names. When a kindergarten student named Alex came to the health room I wanted to make sure that I documented the visit for the correct child. I asked him if he was Alex Johnson. He said, "Just a minute, I have to go look on my desk."

Students were identified on the student database software by last name. A kindergarten student in the health room identified himself as Jacob. I asked him, "What is your other name, Jacob who?" He was quick to tell me his name was not "Jacob Who."

This is what they said….

- A fifth grade student shared with me that he was half Viking and full German.

- A first grade student showed me his library book and announced, "I have a dragon book. It is fiction."

- I was told by a kindergarten student, "I just moved here a long time ago."

- I needed to complete vision screening for a kindergarten student who had been out of school due to illness. I asked her classmate if she was in school today. He said, "No, she is still opposite."

- I was told, "They put my cast on so tight that it's getting loose."

- One student told me about his brother. He explained that they were "brothers since they were born."

- A student with glasses showed me the "blind focals" in her lenses.

- A kindergartner shared that her aunt had a baby girl. "She made it."

- A first grader said his ear pain was because there was a dinosaur in his ear.

- A student who was talking with me about dinosaurs wanted me to know they were now extinct. He thought they "had died in the '80s."

- I had some family pictures in my office. One photo featured the whole clan in matching reunion t-shirts. A student looking at the picture of my family in the re-union t-shirts asked, "Is that you with your soccer team?"

- A second grader told me she was feeling sad because her long-time friend moved away.
    Student: "We were friends for fifteen years?"
    Me: "How old are you?"
    Student: "Eight, but we were friends since we were babies."

- A third grader stopped by the health room. He said he was really excited because, "It's Daylight Savings Time now so we will get out of school an hour earlier."
I didn't have the heart to try and explain.

- Our school clientele was a very mobile population. A third grade boy shared that there were two new students in his class. He expressed some disappointment because, "They are both girls." He continued, "We need another boy, a boy with a dream."

- A student came to the office to ask for help in locating a custodian. He said, "The toilet is full and I am not brave enough to flush it."

- A first grader showed me a picture of a 6" x 2" red rectangle on a piece of paper. "It's called a black snake", he said. He quickly added, "Well, it's not quite black yet."

- I reminded a student to wash his hands. As he turned on the faucet he informed me that the water came all the way from the Atlantic by New York. "That's why it takes a long time for it to come when you turn it on. Before that it wasn't even invented yet."

- A second grader came to the health room and said her stomach hurt. I asked her where it hurt. She said, "In the chair."

Just worried

Often when students would stop by the health room, it became quickly apparent if something was on their mind. A kindergartner came to the health room just as the morning bell rang. She told me she had a bug in her stomach and her stomach hurt when the bug crawled around. She went on to say she went to the hospital yesterday and a nurse there told her that she had a "stomach bug."

One of the students who I rarely saw was brought to the health room by the student support monitor. I was told she complained of chest pain when she got off the bus. Her vital signs were normal, she had no respiratory symptoms, no cardiac history and no history of an injury. She proceeded to say she was worried about her dad. "He is having surgery today. He has something here (taps her upper thigh) they need to fix because my mom keeps getting pregnant."

School Nurse Day

*School Nurse Day is generally celebrated the first
Wednesday in May. School Nurse Day generally
brought several cards from the students.*

Two of my favorite cards:

The front of the card from a second grade student
read, "You are the best school nurse I ever had." The
inside of the card said, "At my last school we didn't
have a school nurse."

Another year the front of a card read, "Happy Nurses
Day," and had a picture of a dog on the card. The
inside of the card said, "You are like my dog
Oscar!!!!" This was followed by an asterisk with a
note that said, "The dog on the front."
(Note: How were Oscar and I alike?????? – I was
afraid to ask!)

What??????

A third grade student came to the health room to show me a bandage on his hand. He said he was bitten by a rabid dog. I asked him how he knew the dog had rabies. He said, "Because it had white stuff coming out of it's mouth." He said his dad took him to the emergency room and now he had to get rabies shots. I called his dad who said that none of this was true. I shared the dad's comment with the student. I asked the student again about being bitten by a dog. He said, "Well, I did get bitten by my pet, but maybe I dreamed the rest."

A student arrived in the health room with a tissue stuck in his nose and said he had a nose bleed. The tissue had no blood on it when it was removed.

Me: "It looks like you fixed your own nose." The student was directed to the sink to wash his hands. I then told him he could return to class.

Student: "My nose is still bleeding."

I examined his nostrils with a light and could not see any active bleeding. I told him that I did not see any bleeding.

Student: "There is never any blood when it bleeds. I have to put tissue in my nose to find it."

After a fall on the playground a student shared that she fell a lot and proceeded to explain: "My legs were born crooked so I fall easily. My mom says they wanted to take them off and put them on right, but she wouldn't let them."

A kindergartner came to the health room to show me a very small piece of loose skin on her right index finger.

Me: "How did this happen?"
Student: "An animal bit me when I got to school."
Me: "What kind of animal?"
Student: "A lady bug."

"OUCH"

Be careful how you ask….

During my nursing education my instructors placed great emphasis on the subjective (what the client said) portion of the nursing assessment. I remember being told that often just by listening carefully the client would lead you to your nursing diagnosis. I found this often to be true. However, I learned early on in my school nurse career that it was important to ask the questions in the right order to avoid prolonged playground stories that hopefully, eventually, related to an injury.

Example 1

A kindergarten girl came to the health room from the playground and was crying. She had no obvious injuries and was walking normally. I opened up the story line floodgate by asking, "What happened?" The girl stopped crying immediately and began her story:

> Well, me and Alisa and Janelle were playing kitties. I was the mommy kitty and they were the baby kitties. Then Tia came and she wanted to play kitties. So then I was the mommy kitty with three baby kitties. I pretended to get milk from a store for them and they were all warm in our kitty house. Then Leah came over and she wanted to play kitties too. But our kitty house was under the slide and there wasn't any more room in our house so we told her she couldn't play kitties with us. She said she wanted to play anyway. It was too crowded in the kitty house and when Leah pushed to get under the slide with the rest of us my shoulder bumped the pole on the slide.

A better first question would have been: "What part of your body is hurt?"

Example 2:

A kindergarten student came from the playground with a stomachache. I soon found out that her stomachache followed some recess disappointment. She explained when her stomachache started hurting.

> We were playing superheroes. I wanted to be Wonder Woman, but Kianna was Wonder Woman. She told me to be Bat Girl. I thought I could be baby Wonder Woman, but she said I couldn't.

(Note: Whose stomach wouldn't hurt after such a letdown??)

Note: The long playground drama stories are not unique to girls. Boys too, have their stories. Just substitute monsters, lizards or a superhero for kitties or Wonder Woman and change a few names and you have the male version of the story.

How did this happen?

- Student with a small rock in his nose: "The wind came up and it just flew in my nose."

- "I was sitting on the carpet and pushed myself over and hit my nose."

- "I want to show you these. The teacher says they are scratches." I told the student that I agreed with the teacher (very superficial scratches). The student said, "I know, but I want to know how I got them."

It's my birthday

I was talking with a fifth grader in the health room toward the end of the school year.

> Student: "Guess when my birthday is? It's coming soon." He went on to say, "It's not May, it's not June……"
>
> Me: "Is it in July?"
>
> Student: "Yes! Guess what day in July. Not the 1st or 2nd or 3rd or 4th or 5th or 6th or 7th or 8th………"
>
> Me: "Is it the 9th?"
>
> Student: "Yes!"
>
> Me: "Aren't I a great guesser?"
>
> Student: "Well, I did give you a few clues."

Moving

Because we frequently had new students enrolling in school, I would often ask students where they moved from. Responses from kindergarten students:

- o "America"
- o "My grandma's"

When a student's tooth came out at school he/she would bring the tooth to the health room for a little storage case and I would make sure any bleeding stopped. I asked one student if the tooth fairy was going to come to his house. He said, "I don't know. This is the first tooth I've lost since moving to a new house."

Communication.........or miscommunication

A kindergarten student had a series of ear infections and the parent sent a note with the student to share that the girl had a referral to an audiologist. The student brought the note to the health room and announced, "I am going to see a meteorologist tomorrow."

Students in our school district were to bring a "Nurse Note" from their teacher when they came to the health room. This provided communication between the teacher and nurse and let staff know where students were going. Occasionally a student arrived without a note. One morning a student without a note arrived and started speaking fast. Trying to clarify what he was saying, I asked, "Are you telling me that you are six or sick?" The student replied emphatically, "I am sick, S-I-K!"

A little girl came to the health room to show me her rash. She said, "My mom thinks it is a heat wave."

A second grader had a history of spastic bladder. This caused urinary urgency and when she had to go to the bathroom, she had to go NOW. One day in physical education the class was playing freeze tag. The student unfortunately had an accident because she was "frozen" and didn't think she could raise her hand to ask to go to the bathroom. We reminded her that she had different rules than the other students.

A student arrived at school late and was wearing sunglasses. School staff told him that sunglasses were not allowed at school. He said he needed to wear the glasses because he had his eyes checked that morning. The eye doctor dilated his eyes and the light bothered his eyes. The boy's father was contacted to verify the story. The father backed his son's story immediately. He said, "Yes, the eye doctor dilated his eyes so that he could look in his eyes to check out his rectum." (Note: That would be <u>retina!</u>)

A third grade student for whom English was a second language told me: "My brother stayed home yesterday because he vomited. I feel nauseous." I asked him what nauseous meant. He said, "I don't remember, maybe dizzy and weak?"

Medication

When children came to the health room complaining of not feeling well, part of the assessment included asking them if they took any medication before coming to school. One student proudly responded, "Yes, and I know the name. It is called 'Take this and you will feel better."

The student arrived at school and immediately came to the health room saying he didn't feel well. I asked him if he had taken any medication this morning. He told me he had taken his "learning pill."

A student arrived in the health room and said, "I need to take my medicine to help me watch the teacher better. I have a hard time doing that. I'm taking HDD."

Health and Human Sexuality

School nurses are often asked to help out with segments of the school Health and Human Sexuality curriculum. A kindergarten student saw me in the hall the day after doing the *Good Touch, Bad Touch* presentation. He proudly told me, "I didn't show anyone my private parts!"

During the question and answer segment of the fourth grade Health and Human Sexuality presentation, one of the boys slowly raised his hand. I called on him and he quietly asked, "Do ALL body parts get bigger?"

When I first began to give classroom presentations for part of the kindergarten Health and Human Sexuality curriculum, I would have a short question and answer session to clarify misconceptions about what was shared. This usually ended up to be a series of stories about topics that were not remotely connected to the presentation. The teachers and I worked with the students to help them understand the difference between a question and a story. I hoped it would help students develop questions about the subject matter. The first question asked after our little session was, "Where do you live?"

I cut out future Q and A segments.

It can be touchy when defining substances that are not healthy for consumption and talking about these substances with pre-school age children. This topic often started a barrage of sharing, i.e., "My dad drinks beer." "My mom smokes cigarettes." It was time for the talk about alcohol. After a brief introduction and some pictures, one of the preschooler's hands suddenly shot up. He said, "Oh, you mean Grandpa Pop!"

What's on your mind
Children going home sick would sometimes start sharing what was on their minds when waiting for a parent to pick them up (WARNING to all adults who are around children!!). One student proceeded to say: "We moved here because my mom wanted an Army guy with a Volvo." I did ask the student how that was working out for her mom. She said, "Not so good."

While waiting for a parent a child mentioned the following: "Me and my sister have different dads. Mom had my sister when she was sixteen, her dad was some dude. Then she got married to my dad and had me."

One student read several books to pass the time while waiting for his ride home. The student eventually started talking about his family and said, "My mom is older than she looks. I think she was drinking lots of coffee, but she quit now."

Wash your hands

It was the time of year to emphasize washing hands and other hygiene measures to avoid flu and colds. I was sharing with a kindergarten class about ways to avoid germs and stay healthy. One student volunteered the following suggestion to help stay healthy, "Take vitamin seeds."

A kindergarten student came to the health room from outdoors to use the bathroom. I did not hear him wash his hands, so as he came out of the bathroom I asked him to go back in to wash his hands.

Student: "I didn't touch any germs."
Me: "You can't see germs so you always need to wash your hands when you go to the bathroom."
Student: "But I don't need to wash my hands because Mother's Day is over."

Health room visits
Stomachaches – a frequent complaint

Student: "Yesterday my head hurt. This morning my stomach hurt."
Me: "What bothers you now?"
Student: "My dog."

A kindergarten student came to the health room around noon complaining of being carsick. I shared that it was lunch time and he had not been in a car for at least four hours. He said, "But I've been in a car lots of times."

A kindergarten student who came to the health room shared that her stomach hurt because she had swallowed some of her own throw up two years ago and it was still bothering her. She continued with her story: "I am never sick with watermelon, I wish I had some of that."
(Note: Sorry. Like most school health rooms, my school did not stock watermelon!)

The primary grades had just finished a unit on nutrition when a kindergartner came to the health room complaining of a stomachache. She said it began to hurt after breakfast.

Me: "What did you eat for breakfast?"

Student: "Something round with frosting and sprinkles."

Me: "Donuts?"

Student: "Yes"

Me: "Did you eat just one?"

Student: "Oh no, my sister said I could eat as many as I wanted. I ate lots."

The student went on to talk about how many donuts she might have eaten when she suddenly stopped in the middle of the sentence and asked, "But wait, what about the food pyramid?"

plate full of donuts

Note: It is always important to find out when the symptoms began.

Student: "I have a headache and a stomachache."
Me: "When did this start?"
Student: "Last night."
Me: "Did you tell your parents?"
Student: "Yes."
Me: "What did they say?"
Student: "Be careful when you run so that you don't fall down."

Student: "I feel like I might throw up."
Me: "When did you start feeling sick?"
Student: "Yesterday."
Me: "What did your mom say about it yesterday?"
Student: "She said to tell my teacher and I just remembered."

In February of 2015:
Student: "I have a headache and a stomachache."
Me: "When did this start?"
Student: "I haven't felt well since 2014."

Student: "I have a headache and a stomachache."
Me: "How long has your head and stomach been hurting?"
Student: "About a week."
Me: "How long is a week?"
Student: "I'm not sure, but I think about 100 days."

Student: "My stomach is hurting."
Me: "When did it start to hurt?"
Student: "The day after today."

Student: "My stomach has hurt since yesterday and I told my dad and mom."
Me: "What did they say?"
Student: "My dad said, 'I love you.'"

Student: "I feel like I am going to vomit and I have a cough."
Me: "When did you start feeling sick?"
Student: "Ever since I got a cut on my foot."
Student takes off his shoe to reveal no cut. "Oh, wrong foot. It is hurting so much it is coming up to my belly."

Student: "I have a stomachache."
Me: "When did your stomach start to hurt?"
Student: "Last night."
Me: "Did you tell your dad or mom?"
Student: "Yes."
Me: "What did they say?"
Student: "Well, my mom did not have any plan. My dad had a plan. He gave me cocoa and said, 'Rest and watch TV.'"

I generally asked students who complained of a stomachache if anyone else in their house was sick. It would give me an idea if a gastrointestinal virus was spreading through the household.

Some responses:

o "My dog."

o "My dad a few days ago. He was out late with some soldiers who made him drink lots of things."
   (Note: Another reminder not to have discussions within earshot of children if you do not want the discussion repeated!!)

- o "My mom got trashed, so she is sick. Now I'm sick. Whatever she gets, I get. It came from her."

- o "Well, my brother has autism, my sister has ringworm, my dad needs to lose weight and my mom has stress. So, everyone has their own issues."

- o "I was throwing up last night and then my sister woke up and she was throwing up and then my dad woke up. Dad said some words that I can't say."

How to describe gastrointestinal ailments

"It started in my side, moved to the middle and then it moved up."

"I threw up but nothing came out."

"I ate syrup this morning and the machine in my stomach stopped working."

"My diarrhea didn't look good. It's not fun when you have diarrhea."

"Sick, like medicine sick last night. My face turned green and I vomited. Oh, wait, I didn't throw up. Let me start over."

"I threw up a real one."

"I drank water a few days ago. It had an ant in it. I think it is still moving around in my stomach."

"After I ate lunch I threw up four icebergs and a cheese spit."

"Feels like it is a house full of food and then a tornado flew around and now it feels like there is a nest in it.

"I threw up four times and I can do it all by myself. I don't need any help."

Headaches

"I felt my forehead and thought I was hot and sick with a headache because I was born in Arizona."

I have a headache because I drank so much water it was higher than my eyes."

"My head hurts because my brain is working too hard."

"My dad had a headache and rubbed my head this morning. I caught his headache."

"My headache started like, BAM. It was like getting shot in the arm. I think a muscle that is generally not there is wrapping around part of my brain."

"My head hurts. My brain is a little loose today."

"I have a headache and a puppy at home."

Colds, ears and noses

A student who looked very tired came to the health room saying he didn't feel good. He explained he "kept boogering too many."

"I got sick this morning when I started snottin' and sneezing."

"I have been coughing every Friday for about a month."

A first grade girl came to the health room because her pierced earring was rubbing the back of her ear. She said, "It hurts and when I blow on something sparks fly out of my ear."

The note from the teacher said the student did not feel well. The student said, "I think I have an ear infection." I looked at the student's ears and throat and listened to her lungs. I told her that I could not find anything that wasn't normal. She said, "Whenever I get my hair fixed and get bows my ears turn the same color."

"All my boogers go down my pipe and it makes me cough."

"I have a runny nose and leaky eyes."

A first grader said, "I've had an earache since I was three or four years old."

Students come to the health room with unique health conditions

A first grade student entered the health room and handed me a note that said, "Eye bothers her." The girl explained, "Sometimes when my mom comes to wake me up in the morning my eye is stuck shut and I can't hear her."

"When I take a deep breath it feels bumpy."

"I was walking down the hall and everything seemed pitch white."

"I haven't been breathing much at school the past few days."

A kindergarten student told me that he had a case of the "tired bones." He then immediately collapsed on the floor to demonstrate.

"I was eating pizza and started having a heart attack. I only like cheese pizza. Oh, and the fingers on my right hand hurt."

"I picked the scab off so now it's drowning."

A kindergarten student who had wet shorts because he hadn't made it to the bathroom in time explained, "The pee zoomed out of me."

"I haven't felt well all day. My temperature this morning was 180!"

A student with a raspy voice told me, "My throat beat me because I didn't take a shower."

"My voice hurts."

So bad I can't remember

"My foot has been bothering me really bad since last night." The student took off his shoe to show me. There was no sign of any injury to his foot and no sign of pain with palpation. He said, "I can't remember which one it is, let me check the other one."

"My leg hurts from walking yesterday." The student rubbed his left knee to show where it hurt. I shared with the student that the note from the teacher said when he was in class he was rubbing his right knee and complaining of pain.
He said, "Oh, I guess I got mixed up."

A first grader came to the health room from the playground. He complained of pain by his right shoulder. He said his shoulder was bumped when he fell. I did notice a small scrape on his left shoulder and some dust on his shirt. I shared this with him. He said, "Well, one of my shoulder hurts, I just can't remember which one."

"I fell out of my chair because of a cramp in my leg right here." The student pointed to an area over his right shin. I advised the student that it's rare to get a cramp there because there isn't much muscle there. He said, "Oh, I forgot, it was in my arm."

A third grade student came to the health room to tell me that his ear hurt "REALLY BAD."

Student: "It feels like a bump. Is it a zit?"
Me: "Yes."
Student: "Would you write a note to my mom so I won't forget to tell her?"
Me: "Why would you forget to tell your mom if it is hurting so bad?"
Student: No response.

Planning ahead

A kindergarten student came to the health room and said, "I threw up two times." I asked her if this happened today. She said, "No, next week I think."

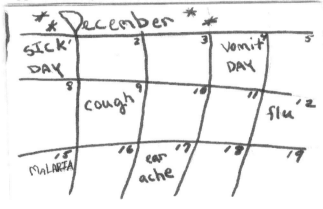

A student came to the health room requesting an ice pack. I asked her why. She said, "I bumped my leg yesterday, but you weren't here. I need ice because I might bump it again."

A fifth grader came to the health room following lunch. He said he needed to "go home and get ready to be sick." I shared that this was quite a strategic plan. He said, "You have to expect the unexpected."

Kindergarten Student: "I feel like I am going to puke."
Me: "Did you puke?"
Kindergarten Student: "No, but I will if you want me to."

I asked a student who complained of a stomachache if she had vomited. She said, "I think so." I told her that she either did vomit or she didn't vomit. She should know. She replied, "Well not today, but maybe next week. My mom said I could."

Students would often stop in the health room to show me an old injury. (I guess just for reassurance???) Anyway, a kindergarten student came to show me a very old cut on her foot. I asked her when it happened. She said, "Tomorrow."

Injuries

I was putting a small amount of petroleum jelly on a bandage before applying it to a small superficial scrape on a student's knee. She asked, "What's the sauce for?"

Even though the student had a small scrape on her knee she assured me that it hurt "BAD". She said, "If it burns anymore it will be like lava squirting out."

A fourth grade student came to the health room holding her left arm at a right angle. She told me she broke her arm last week because she held a one-year-old baby for an hour (she had been fine until a math test was scheduled to begin).

A fifth grade student came to the health room saying he got hurt playing chess. He could not tell me where the injury was and I could not find one!

A kindergarten student requested a bandage for her fingernail because the tip of it was loose. I applied a bandage and told the student she could return to class. She said, "I was hoping to sit down and rest and relax my finger for a while before going back to my class."

Invisible problems

"I fell and have a scratch on my arm, right here. But you can't see it."

A student with a very small amount of blood on his knee came in from the playground. He washed his knee and there was no laceration or abrasion on his knee. He immediately said, "Well now it doesn't look that serious."

"I have an invisible rash that is all over my body. It was worse before. It is getting better now."

A student came in daily to apply ointment to his skin for treatment of eczema. While in the health room he said the bathroom door shut on his arm and he requested an ice pack to put on it. I asked him which arm was hurt as there was no mark of any kind on either arm. He replied, "I can't remember."

"I have a bruise over here…..now here. It must have moved again. It is traveling all over my body." (It moved very quickly, neither the student nor I ever saw it!)

A second grade student came to the health room scratching behind her knee and said she had a rash. She had jeans on and pulled her pant leg up to show me the rash. There was no rash or redness. She said, "My rash sometimes gets scared when I go to see a nurse and disappears."

Vision and hearing screening
To test if a student's eyes converge symmetrically, a small target (toy) is slowly brought toward the student's nose. Repeating this up to three times can cause the eye muscles to tire and muscle weakness might become apparent if the eyes don't track well. As I was doing this screening with a first grade student he asked me, "Are you trying to hypnotize me?"

Another screening tool, Plus Lens, is used to detect excessive far-sightedness. The procedure involves having the student put on special lenses and attempt to read a regular eye chart. Students who can read the chart while wearing these lenses fail the screening. When I placed the lenses on one of the students he said, "It doesn't look like the language I speak." That would be a PASS.

I noticed that a student I was to screen had new eyeglasses. I asked him about his glasses. He said, "The doctor gave me these glasses. I need to wear them until my eyes change color."

Our school district generally did kindergarten vision screening with a tool that didn't require the student to identify letters. To pass this screening a student had only to identify which of four pictures (girl, boy, rabbit or bird) the "tumbling E's" were pointing to (We called them table legs). Even though this is a simple screening tool, I had to prepare the kindergarten students for this new (to them) test. I would go into the classroom prior to screening the students and spend time showing them samples of what they were going to see (girl, boy, rabbit, bird), reviewing expectations and having them practice their response. The first student accompanied me to the screening area after this preparation phase. She assured me she knew what she was to do so I showed her the first slide.

Me: "Can you see the picture?"
Student: "Yes, easy."
Me: "What picture are the table legs pointing to?"
Student: "A turtle."

(A turtle? So much for my great screening orientation!!!)

When doing vision screening it is always important to screen each eye. After changing the eye cover from the left eye to the right eye, the preschooler closed both of his eyes. He told me he wanted to see if he could see the chart with both eyes closed.

A student was blinking excessively and squinting when trying to identify letters on the eye chart.

> Student: "I see two of each letter when I look at it. This always happens."
> Me: "Have you told your dad or mom this happens?"
> Student: "I told my mom."
> Me: "What did your mom say?"
> Student: "That's spooky."

(Note- The student did get glasses.)

After failing the vision screening a student told me he got his eyes checked at the eye doctor in town. He proceeded to say, "The doctor said I'm nearsighted. I think I caught it from my cousin. He has it too."

A first grader was called to the office to complete hearing screening. She came to the office and asked, "Where do I go to get my ears pierced?"

I was orienting a new nurse and demonstrating the procedure for hearing screening. She practiced screening my hearing. The next step was to screen some of the students. I said: "Hopefully, tomorrow we can pull in a couple guinea pigs for you to screen." This got the attention of a student who was resting on one of the health room cots. He looked confused and said, "You put those headphones on guinea pigs?!"

Nurse Notes from teachers
*Probably after a particularly **long** day*

Nurse Call

Date _____ Time 2:00
Student Name My Mayla
Teacher _____
Phone 1-800-IAM-SICK

COMPLAINT

Headache _____ Stomach ache ✓
Sore Throat _____ ✓ Earache ✓
Nausea/Vomiting ✓ Diarrhea _____
Congestion/Cough _____ Rash _____
Other _____

ACTION TAKEN

Temp _____ Rest _____ Cool Pack _____
Parental Contact _____
Unable to Contact Parent _____
Left Message at Home/Work _____
Other _____

Time Back To Class _____
Home _____

Nurse Call

Date _____
Student Name John Time 12:15
Teacher _____
Phone _____

COMPLAINT

Headache _____
Sore Throat _____ Stomach ache _____
Nausea/Vomiting _____ Earache _____
Congestion/Cough _____ Diarrhea _____
Other _____ Rash _____

Leg fell off ✓

ACTION TAKEN Needs
Temp _____ Rest _____ Cool Pack *Bandaid!*
Parental Contact _____
Unable to Contact Parent _____
Left Message at Home/Work _____
Other _____

Time Back To Class _____
Home _____

Working Together with Parents

Have you ever had a situation, where in that moment, you wish you could have a "do-over" on the last 30 minutes of your life? It is only in reflecting after a period of time (some require a considerable amount of time) that you can see the levity of the situation. Well here is one of mine!

The start of a new school year brought with it a new assignment. I was tasked to be the school nurse for three elementary schools with a combined enrollment of about nine hundred students.

The schools were only about five miles apart so I visited them each daily. I was at each building only about two hours a day. This made it difficult to get to know many of the students.

The school secretaries provided health care to students in my absence. Each time I arrived at a building a secretary would quickly fill me in on what happened in my absence and I would pick up from there.

One day when I arrived at my second building for the day, the secretary told me there was a first grade student in the health room waiting to see me. She said the student had a stomachache and didn't feel like she could return to her class.

I proceeded with my "stomachache assessment." I felt that the student could return to class, but the student did not agree. My next move in this situation was to contact a parent and let the student and parent decide if the student would return to class or if the parent wished to pick up the student from school.

I called the mother on the contact list, no answer. The father answered his phone and I explained the situation to him. I then handed the phone to the student so they could speak. She listened and periodically said, "Yes sir", and then hung up on the call before I could speak with the parent. She immediately said she was okay and returned to her class.

After clearing off some paperwork on my desk I walked out to the front desk to ask the secretaries if there was anything else I needed to be aware of. They said, "No", and asked if the first grader returned to class. I told them she talked with her dad and returned to class. They looked surprised and shared that there was no father in this girl's life. It was then that I found out something VERY interesting about the first grade. One first grade teacher had two students in her classroom that had the <u>same</u> first name, the <u>same</u> last name and the <u>same</u> date of birth!

I quickly went back to the health room and pulled out the files for the "name alikes". You guessed it. I had called the wrong parent!

Well, now to undo the misunderstanding.

I contacted the student's real mom first. What an interesting conversation might have ensued if the student went home and told her mom she spoke with her dad on the phone while at school!! The mother graciously accepted my apology and said she would speak with her daughter about it. Yea, one down.

Now to return a call to the father I had contacted (It was during this second call that I found out this soldier was deployed in the Middle East!). Luckily, he thought the whole situation was humorous. He said he thought it was unusual that his daughter was saying, "Yes sir." (Some military dependents are taught to respond this way so I didn't think it was unusual. I obviously didn't know his daughter.)

He had a good laugh about it. Perhaps it was a nice break from his regular daily tasks. I asked him what he said to the student because as soon as she hung up the phone she immediately returned to class. He said he told her to, "Suck it up and go back to class!"

I shared with him that some days there were students who were struggling to stay in class. I jokingly asked if it would it be okay if I kept his number on speed dial to call in these situations. He just laughed and said it would be great!

I can say it is a funny situation now, especially since the parents were so understanding. However, as you might expect, at that moment I found no humor in what had happened!

And last, but definitely important!
A note from a parent on her son's
health enrollment form:

"He is not taking any medication right now. If you find out what is wrong with him, please call me."

Made in the USA
San Bernardino, CA
09 December 2019

61129325R00031